DOGS UNLEASHED

From On-Leash To Off-Leash

Leash Training for Dog Lovers

Tim Carter

Founder MyGermanShepherd.Org

Edition 3

Disclaimer

Every dog is special, through its unique genetical heritage, living environment, and personal treatment by its owner or handler, as well as prior and current human and animal contacts.

Accordingly, no suggestions given to a dog owner or handler can ever be right for every dog and its owner regardless of the individual circumstances. It is your and your dog's individual circumstances that may or may not make a certain form of training, care, or remedy successful in your case.

You are encouraged to consciously observe your puppy and adult dog in order to recognize any adverse development as soon as possible, and to apply your own common sense to complement the suggestions made in this book, in light of your individual situation.

Neither the publisher nor the author can be held accountable, neither for the favorable implications of applying any suggestion made in this book, nor for the unfavorable implications. It is your dog's individual situation that will determine the success of any and every suggestion made in this book, and your dog's individual situation as well as your opinion will change with time.

DEDICATION

This Leash Training Guide is dedicated to
liberal dog owners who want to
<u>make the leash the last resort</u>

Unchain your dog - unchain your heart

Contents

The Goal

While for most dog trainers and book authors the goal with Leash Training is 'no more pulling' or 'perfect heeling', for us here this is not the goal - these are mere *side effects* that will be achieved automatically.

Instead, our goal with Leash Training is to <u>replace the leash with the Recall</u>. To <u>make the leash the last resort</u>. As it should be.

Why?

Look: What is the purpose of putting a dog on-leash if we can call our dog reliably to us, and the dog stays with us until we give the cue to release the dog? Exactly. In all such cases, the leash becomes irrelevant.

Since you got this book as a **dog lover** (see the book title), you too hopefully don't want to subject your dog to an <u>unnecessary restraint</u>, right?

In fact, the typical leash walk harms behavior and health of both dog and owner.

What did he just say??

The typical leash walk *harms* behavior and health of both dog *and* owner:

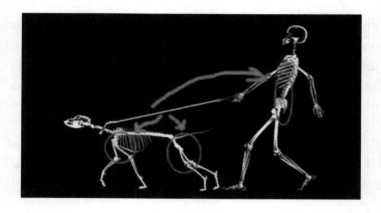

The typical leash walk is that dog owners (and even professional dog trainers!) walk their dog on a <u>tight leash</u>. Or rather, the dog walks the owner. The dog pulls so much and so abrupt that the owner may fall over or strains the shoulder, elbow, wrist joint, or back, and is in agony! Can you relate?

All seen countless times with my own eyes. Plus, at <u>mygermanshepherd.org</u> we get a LOT of 'dog problem' reports from members and visitors alike (German Shepherds have *enormous* pull power!) - and even if the dog owner doesn't mention a leash problem, I can conclude from the other reported problems that the owner has a leash problem too.

The typical leash walk ruins both the dog's *and* the owner's joints, muscles, ligaments, and tendons - <u>and nerves</u>! Plus, it stresses out the dog (and us). Stress leads to aggression. The typical leash walk makes the dog aggressive (and us too).

You may not notice this - but you will notice how *relaxed* you are in a few days if you start our Leash Training here TODAY.

What the leash walk should do is, make the dog *calm*. Relax the dog. And us too.

However, what many dog owners who send us their help requests at first don't accept is the fact that Leash Training - like every other goal of dog training - requires to start the training with things the dog owner doesn't want to hear about: Because (s)he believes they have nothing to do with the current problem.

But they have *everything* to do with it. To be successful with dog training, with stopping the dog from pulling on the leash or whatever, we *must* address the source of the problem, not the symptom.

Here, the symptom is 'leash pulling' or 'not heeling', but the source is that the dog has not *accepted* you as Pack leader. What *you* think you are, is meaningless to a dog. If the dog hasn't *accepted* you as Pack leader, you will have a very hard time to get from your dog the behavior you want.

Conversely, once you are your dog's *accepted* Pack leader, dog training feels like a walk in the park (without leash)! It becomes *easy*.

If and when we walk our dog *on-leash*, the leash will never be tight, we only walk with a loose leash. We don't do a single step while the leash is tight!

The right Leash Training allows us to walk our dog *off-leash* most of the time, and when we need the dog close by, we CALL the dog to us, and the dog reliably comes and stays with us until we give the release cue.

This is the final outcome of the right Leash Training. Anything else is kindergarden. Let's agree here and now: You and I, we both have grown out of kindergarden. If you feel you haven't - regarding dog training ;-) - there are enough less demanding Leash Training books on offer in your favorite bookstore.

In my view, a leash has no other purpose than to restrain a dog that otherwise you cannot restrain. Mark that. Once again:

> A leash has no other purpose than to restrain a dog that otherwise you cannot restrain

'You' is the dog owner or dog trainer. Thus I find it *odd*, to say the least, when professional dog trainers have to walk their dog everywhere *on-leash*! Something in their training must have gone wrong, no?

A dog that can only be restrained with a leash,
this is a *poor* training outcome!

Brief Note on Links

In the prior chapter there was already a link. Thus let me briefly mention this, in case you don't know the practice on our website and in my other books.

Throughout the entire book the focus is on helping you through relevant links, like we do on our breed authority site mygermanshepherd.org - the largest in the world.

Book-internal links

The abundance of cross-links should allow you to use this Leash Training guide as **reference guide**, moving around as you like.

Book-external links

Many of these links lead to additional content for you (to keep the book slim for those who want a quick read). These links lead to our (normally members-only) *Periodicals*, most of which are extensively researched and comprehensive discussions of a specific topic. That's why I decided to link the extra content, such that whenever you want, you can visit the linked webpages at your own choice to deepen your understanding.

Obviously, the linked Periodicals are helpful to you regardless which breed of dog or mix you have - *unless* we specifically state in one of those Periodicals that a certain point relates to the German Shepherd dog only. So, *do* make use of all the additional linked Periodicals, because they give you incredible more value above and beyond the limited space in this book. Okay?

All other external links are to <u>remedies</u> or articles on other websites. In case of remedy links, most of the time these point to Amazon, namely whenever Amazon offers the item *and* is the cheapest source (which is generally the case since they have the biggest buying power globally, and many vendors use Amazon as sales platform for their own items).

Note that the majority of dog products are being developed and marketed where the majority of pet dogs live: 78 million in the USA! Hence our default remedy links point to amazon.<u>com</u> (and I have done the same in this book). But what if you live in Canada, or you want to gift the item to your sister in the UK who has a dog too?

Then you would need to get the <u>eBook</u>, which uses cute flags to help you find the right item in any Amazon locale (so many links wouldn't be possible in a print book). Thus, instead of say:

<u>Nutramax Dasuquin with MSM</u> (mygermanshepherd .org/go/nutramax-msm) - which is without doubt the *top* remedy for dog mobility problems -

...the eBook would show: <u>Nutramax Dasuquin with MSM</u> ▨ ▣ ▬ ▬ ▮ ▮ ▮ (like we do it on our website). The links embedded in each cute flag give eBook readers the freedom to choose their preferred supplier (I love freedom). Nice side effect: The flags also lighten up the text and they document that our world is increasingly interconnected - certainly for dogs.

Special Note for the Print Edition

Obviously with a print book the biggest disadvantage is that you cannot simply click on a linked word or image to jump to another book location, or to see the linked remedies, articles, or our site's Periodicals.

To give you access to the book-internal cross-references and linked extras nonetheless, I have painstakingly added page numbers and web addresses (URLs) to the relevant text locations. Took me ages, but I expect it will help you enormously when you seek more detail in future. Just note that due to the print process the page references can get slightly off track.

All URLs have hard line breaks, so that you can type them exactly as you see them (just without the line break). Example: mygermanshepherd.org/go/stypti c-powder

Please accept that all other hyphenation in this book is done automatically by Microsoft Word.

The Mindset

Remember, *our* goal here with Leash Training is to **replace the leash with the Recall**. This requires that, even *before* we start Leash Training, we develop a certain <u>mindset</u>:

In dog training, <u>our mindset</u> is
the overall key to success

Why?

Because our mindset determines our mood and energy state - and dogs are <u>energy recipients</u>! Meaning, dogs assume the energy state of their owner or handler within seconds.

So often dog owners complain: "But ...xyz... isn't working with my dog, she's *different!*"

No, it isn't working with the dog owner, *she's* different. She doesn't adapt her mindset first. Then her dog training cannot work. Then a cat would be more suitable (cats are energy donors, thus our mindset is irrelevant when training a cat).

What mindset?

Relaxed

If we want a <u>calm dog</u> during our walks (and beyond) then we <u>must</u> be relaxed ourselves whenever we engage with our dog. There is no way around this, because dogs are energy recipients.

I can't stress this enough:

Our own state of mind <u>fundamentally impacts</u> our dog's behavior and health!

Even when you are just strolling along with your dog on the leash (or off-leash), your state of *mind* <u>will</u> impact on your dog's *behavior*.

———

Odd: I only now(!) realize that this might sound to some like I am one of those "water can think" *new age psychedelics*. No, far from it. I am scientist through and through.

The centered statement above has nothing to do with being 'psychedelic', it has to do with simple science. Since this is a **Leash Training Guide**, I'll try to explain the above in just 3 bullet points. They describe a much *simplified* situation only for clarity. The explanation is likewise true for more complex situations:

- Say we are *upset*, then our blood pressure rises, the chemistry in the transpiration on our skin changes, and body posture and movements change too

- The modern domesticated dogs are the result of targeted breeding to make them extremely *sociable*, ie to use all their senses to *observe* us, and then to *adapt*

- When our dog observes (olfactory, auditory, and visually) that we are *upset*, the dog adapts!

Dogs always adapt to the energy state ('mood') of their human carer. Always!

When dog owners or trainers argue "I have such an aggressive dog!", I ask them "Have you considered how relaxed you are in your life? Thus how relaxed you come across to your dog?"

Of course there are dogs that are very aggressive when we first meet them (like there are other dogs that are very calm, peaceful, and playful). But the point is: Dogs aren't *born* aggressive, they *become* aggressive. Primarily:

1. when they are kept on a high energy level for far too long

2. when they have been treated badly

3. when they are traumatized from some prior experience

4. when they are not well hydrated.

The above are the primary <u>causes</u> of aggression (and seemingly in that very order!). The <u>symptoms</u> of dog aggression then are:

- Dog on Dog aggression
- Dominance aggression (dog thinks it is Pack leader)
- Territorial aggression (again, dog thinks it is Pack leader)
- Fear aggression
- Food aggression
- or **Leash aggression**

Thus if you know your dog is hyperactive on the leash, before you do anything else, consider your own energy level (state of mind), and aim to *relax*, before you even leave the house for the dog walk!

Benevolent

In addition to being <u>relaxed</u> (p~20), it is very helpful to be **benevolent** when we train our dog, because I would argue that dogs *feel* how well we mean it with them.

Proof: With certain measures of **Dog Care** - see for example <u>Mouth Care</u> (mygermanshepherd.org/perio dical/gsd-mouth-care), <u>Ear Care</u> (mygermanshephe rd.org/periodical/gsd-ear-care), <u>Eye Care</u> (mygerm anshepherd.org/periodical/gsd-eye-care), and <u>Paw Care</u> (mygermanshepherd.org/periodical/gsd-paw-care) as well as **Dog Health** - see for example <u>Dental Disease</u> (mygermanshepherd.org/my-germ an-shepherd/german-shepherd-health/german-shep herd-dental-disease-or-gum-inflammation) and <u>Skin Infection</u> (mygermanshepherd.org/my-german-shep herd/german-shepherd-health/german-shepherd-ba cterial-skin-infection) we need to do things that our dog will not like at all. If a stranger did those things, any dog would outright bite that person! However, when <u>we</u> do those things, our dog will wince but not bite us.

This is so if our dog knows from past experience that we always had in mind to <u>help</u> the dog. That we never punished or threatened our dog. Dogs for sure have such consciousness, see for example Stanley Coren's <u>The Intelligence of Dogs: Canine Con-sciousness and Capabilities</u> (mygermanshepherd.org /go/book-intelligence-of-dogs-consciousness).

Confident

Canines have a genetically ingrained *quest* to belong to a Pack. Dogs *need* a Pack to live and thrive. And domesticated dogs need a *human* Pack to live and thrive, they need us to keep mentally healthy. This is unique in the animal world, as far as I know. Or do *you* know of any animal that *needs* us humans in order to feel calm and relaxed?

BUT: Dogs' genetic heritage also requires them to strive for Pack *leadership*, as I mentioned before. Despite all the targeted breeding of domesticated dogs over the last 33,000 years(!), breeders haven't been able (or haven't desired) to eliminate this inherent canine quest - which is a remnant of having wolves as distant ancestors.

(Again, some people waste their life-time discussing whether wolves *do* seek leadership of their pack if there is no clear leader. Had they just watched one wolf documentary from Attenborough & Co they would be doing something else with their life - maybe reading this book)

Anyway, the inherited quest of domesticated dogs to strive for Pack leadership is why timid dog owners feel dominated by their dog. If we let them, dogs will walk us, instead of us walking the dog! This applies to all the dog owners that you see on the street, on TV, in videos, and on photos who are being *dragged* down the road by their dog. - You'll see one such dog owner in a moment, and you may recognize him. ;-)

If you don't want this, being *dragged* down the road, then you *must* show **confidence**. You *must* demonstrate confident Pack leadership, each day anew - or your dog will soon rule over you.

I am serious here. Don't be timid with your dog. But don't be a 'commander' either, see next.

Partner

A final, fourth characteristic of the <u>Mindset</u> (p~19) we need for our Leash Training (like for all dog training), is that of a 'Partner'.

With 'Partner' I mean the opposite of a 'Master-Servant' mindset - because that is what we must <u>not</u> practice if we want that our dog walks calm on the leash, comes back when we call, and heels when we want our dog to stay close by. The whole concept of 'obedience' is leading dog owners on the wrong path.

With the 'Partner' mindset, we will *command* our dog less, and *lead* more - <u>with or without the lead</u>. We become the *accepted* Pack leader, not the commander!

―――――――――――

There is much more I could say (and actually have said) about all of this. The above may not be enough for *every* reader to understand the gravity of our mindset for our dog training (a few people always complain...), but since this is no more than a **Leash Training** Guide, the above must suffice.

More about the right Mindset and other Dog Training Tools is in the <u>Dog Training Toolkit</u> (my germanshepherd.org/go/dog-training-toolkit).

Something Else We Need...

For entirely successful Leash Training as presented in this book, we need something else, in addition to the right <u>Mindset</u> (p~19): We need to become our dog's *accepted* Pack leader (p~14). We need to mitigate <u>the conflict our dog is experiencing in its Pack</u>.

In short (ultrashort): Dogs struggle with their perceived role as Pack leader. From the owner's behavior (that's you, me, or any other dog owner), the dog partly gets the impression that (s)he is the Pack leader: The dog can do what (s)he wants to get our attention, and - if we've got a large dog - (s)he may even *drag us behind* on a leash!

However, <u>the conflict</u> arises because naturally any dog struggles with this role. Every day, maybe every hour. Because, in countless situations the dog has to experience that (s)he is not the *accepted* Pack leader:

- The owner always <u>commands</u> the dog around, inside and outside of the house

- The owner decides over the <u>walk</u> by opening the door or leaving it closed

- The owner even puts a collar around the dog's <u>neck</u>(!), and keeps the dog on a leash - and pulls, tears, and drags the dog via the connection leash - collar - neck - throat!

- Worst of all, the owner determines when, what, and how much <u>food</u> the dog gets to eat!

All this and much more, makes clear to the dog that it has to continue to prove its leader status in the family Pack - like the dog would do in the wild - until (s)he is the <u>accepted</u> Pack leader, or until (s)he is outperformed by another Pack leader. In this case: Us!

This permanent conflict puts enormous **stress** on the dog. Stress leads to health and behavior problems. Foremost, stress leads to **aggression**.

Now you will appreciate *why*, according to <u>CDC</u> (US Centers for Disease Control and Prevention), in the USA alone, at least *4.7 million* people are <u>bitten</u> by dogs every year! And why I already stated on p~21 as the <u>Number ONE cause of aggression</u>: "when they are kept on a high energy level for far too long". This high energy level results from <u>the conflict the dog is experiencing in its pack</u>!

So, in short: We need to become our dog's *accepted* Pack leader, to mitigate the conflict our dog is experiencing in its Pack.

This goes way beyond Leash Training. I will not inflate this **Leash Training Guide** further with such *general* dog training skill. The shortest introduction to becoming the *accepted* Pack leader you get with the Dog Lover's Summary Reference Guide: Adult Dog Training IN A NUTSHELL (my germanshepherd.org/go/adult-dog-nutshell) - or if you have a puppy, Puppy Training IN A NUTSHELL (mygermanshepherd.org/go/puppy-nutshell).

More comprehensive guidance is for example in the Puppy Development Guide - Puppy 101 (mygerm anshepherd.org/go/puppy-development-guide) and in the Complete House Training Guide (mygerma nshepherd.org/go/house-training-guide). **House Training** is by far the largest part of all dog training, hence I have included 'Pack conflict and Pack leadership' there).

Alternatively, the key means how to become the *accepted* Pack leader are explained in the (normally members-only) free Periodical on our website: Dog Meals - Meal Times - and Feeding Routine (mygerm anshepherd.org/periodical/dog-meals-meal-times-and-feeding-routine). While it may not seem so, really these are the key means! Although the Periodical is written for German Shepherd dog owners, the principles equally apply to any other dog breed or mix you may have.

A final prerequisite for entirely successful Leash Training is the right **Socialization** - we will get back to this at the end of the book.

The Right Equipment

In addition to the right _Mindset_ (p~19) and becoming the _accepted_ Pack leader (p~27), we need some physical equipment. We need:

- two collars (outdoor and indoor)

- the outdoor collar with ID tag

- a short leash

- a long leash

- and if desired, a harness.

Do we need Food Treats? No. A clear: NO! Quite the opposite: If you use food treats for your dog training, I can almost guarantee that you will never reach the training goal we have with this book: To **replace the leash with the Recall**.

Why?

1. A dog that comes for your treats does not come for you

2. A dog that does not come for you has not accepted you as Pack leader

3. When you are not the _accepted_ Pack leader, you will have a very hard time to train your dog anything beyond the basics

4. To be able to train your dog *anything* you <u>must</u> become your dog's *accepted* Pack leader!

5. Once you are your dog's *accepted* Pack leader, <u>food treats are irrelevant</u>

Considering how many dog trainers tell you that, for dog training, you need a <u>treat pouch</u> filled with tasty morsels, you may not *believe* me here. But you got this book now anyway. So: Give it a serious try. Then you will see: It works.

Thousands of dog owners have rejoiced over our dog training skill at mygermanshepherd.org - because they gave it a serious try. So: Forget about food treats! I call that 'treat training'. Save your money, and your dog's love.

Two Collars

For a dog and a puppy alike, <u>the collar is the most essential safekeeping equipment</u> - more important than the leash, the ID tag, flea- and tick prophylaxis, and vaccinations.

When your dog would have the *chance* to get outside, the collar should stay on all the time. Obviously this is for safety reasons, but also for training purposes: Unless your dog is miraculously well behavior-trained, there will come situations when you need to be able to <u>walk to</u> your dog and take hold of the collar. Not to pull or even drag the dog somewhere, just to *gently* take hold of the collar. If our dog doesn't wear a collar, we have nothing to hold on to *gently*.

Certainly with a puppy,
the collar must stay on <u>all the time</u>,
and with an adult dog, at the very least
whenever the dog has a *chance* to get outside

This is what dog owners typically get with a new dog:

Bestselling puppy and dog collar (mygermansh epherd.org/go/puppy-collar) - available in all sizes from 6 to 28 inch

Note: Always measure your dog's neck girth at the *narrowest* point of the neck. If you measure at the base of the neck, as often recommended, sooner or later you'll end up with that common issue that the dog pulled the collar over its ears and ... it's gone! Hopefully only the collar, not the dog.

Thus measure at the *narrowest* point, and then add a small finger width (for small dogs) up to twice middle finger width (for large dogs).

For <u>toy breeds and small puppies</u> up to 14 inch neck girth the above collar indeed is a great collar. So why then are there complaints (amzn.to/1cosbLB) about this collar?

Obviously because its cheap price reflects its quality: It's made of nylon with single stitching, cheap buckle and cheap print. Once you use a collar like this on a mid-size or large dog (14 to 28 inch neck girth), in addition to the print coming off, the buckle soon breaks, and the nylon tears.

Further, the above collar is not the ideal stay-on collar: The nylon and the buckle are somewhat uncomfortable for a dog. Much better than a plastic, metal chain, choke or prong collar, but nonetheless not the best.

The stay-on collar, to be worn inhouse and particularly at night, should be the most comfortable available - because we want a *calm* dog, to avoid unnecessary behavior issues.

The most comfortable collar is a **soft padded genuine leather collar** with flat-on buckle:

Bestselling leather collar (mygermanshepherd.org/go/bestselling-leather-collar) - in sizes from 11 to 23 inch

If you don't believe this, you may want to try on different collars yourself: Wear a leather, a nylon, a plastic, a metal chain, a choke, and a prong collar, each for one day. Although I am not 100% serious (I am rarely), I can guarantee that afterwards you will know exactly which type of collar you want to get for your dog, if you are a **dog lover** (see the book title).

Soft padded genuine leather collars like the one above provide a feel-good factor that synthetic collars (and certainly chain, choke, and prong collars) cannot provide.

Now, depending on where, when, and how we walk our dog, we may want to get a <u>second collar</u>:

- If the dog is out at night
- or in heavy or frequent rain
- or swims once a while

then a leather collar is not ideal. For outdoors, generally a reflective water-resistant collar is best, and these usually are not made of leather (this is why I wrote above "we need *two* collars").

The top reflective water-resistant collar is made of nylon with safety buckle and comes from Rogz in various colors:

<u>Rogz reflective outdoor dog collar</u> (mygermansh epherd.org/go/rogz-reflective-dog-collar), in sizes from 13 to 22 inch

Here we see that a cheap price doesn't necessarily mean it's bad quality: The Rogz collar is cheaper than the collar shown in the beginning, and nonetheless it's better quality.

I personally always seek the best quality at a low price, and I assume you do the same. Although there are a few lemons with *every* brand (even say Mercedes-Benz), getting the lemon should be the rare exception, not the rule.

Harness

Some dog lovers don't like to subject their dog to a **collar**, and I can fully understand this: The mere thought of having my own *neck* tied up makes me shudder!

A **harness** I would find much more comfortable, and I can assume, so does our dog. Strangely then, some people don't like a harness for their dog:

- "A harness is cruel, inhumane"

Well, a harness restrains the dog around the entire chest, instead of at the neck. So, isn't a harness in fact much more humane/canine? I should say so. If you doubt this, try on both, a harness and a collar, and feel for yourself.

- "A harness is not suitable to restrain a strong dog"

There it is! So, that's their true worry!

If your dog pulls on the leash, you have a Leash Training problem, not a harness problem. In fact, with a strong dog, I'd *recommend* that you get a harness, as this will motivate you to give more attention to the right Leash Training.

In the moment when the dog pulls (or *you* pull), a harness that <u>fits well</u> is much more calming to the dog than a collar, *regardless* how well the collar fits. And in all other moments, when the dog *doesn't* pull, a harness that fits well is as comfortable as a collar that fits well.

I feel that, particularly with a strong dog, dog owners prefer a <u>collar</u> for their dog only because it's *more effective* in restraining the dog: Once the dog can hardly breathe, the pulling weakens.

But you know what happens then? The shortness of oxygen makes the dog even *more agitated*, because in addition, the dog is now fighting for survival. Worse: The dog owner's *counterforce* makes the situation *more memorable*. The dog owner just *trained* the dog to pull, so the dog will do exactly that more often now!

You may want to <u>read the last paragraph again</u>, because I fear that despite the emphasis laid on individual words I couldn't relate the gravity of what I just said.

What you read above is a <u>fundamental training insight</u> (not only relating to dog training, human training too):

The higher the energy state (here agitated pulling and then your counterforce on top), the better the dog will remember (here: to pull).

While we humans think: "My counterforce showed the dog that I don't want him/her to pull upon such stimulus!" (squirrel, cat, dog, motorbiker, whatever) - the dog thinks: "This thing [excited/scared/upset] my Pack buddy/leader too, next time I'll raise the alarm sooner/more!"

If your dog pulls you on the leash, you don't need a more effective physical restraint, but a more effective *trained* restraint. You need exactly **this Leash Training Guide**. As you will see here in a moment, there should be **zero pulling** when you walk your dog.

Don't wait for the dog to pull to train the dog *not* to pull, that would be too late. To train the dog *not* to pull, this must be done before you even walk your dog where (s)he *might* pull.

Like with the collar, if you get a harness then get the most comfortable one. It doesn't have to be 'the mother of all harnesses' from Dean & Tyler (mygermanshepherd.org/go/dog-harness):

Unless your dog is strong, the cheap bestselling harness from Puppia pictured before does a great job (mygermanshepherd.org/go/dog-harness-cheap).

The key benefit of a harness is that the dog doesn't feel strangled at the *throat/neck*. A harness is much more gentle on your dog.

But again, when back inside, better put on a light soft padded leather collar like the one shown on p~36. Such a collar you can leave on all the time without much bothering the dog.

Also note that a soft but snug-fit harness like the Dean & Tyler or the Puppia can do part of the job of a <u>thundershirt</u> (mygermanshepherd.org/go/thundershirt) in <u>treating canine anxiety</u>. Indeed, let's look at this right now.

Why Dogs Pull

Let's look at this now because when we understand *why* dogs pull, it helps us with our overall dog training, not just Leash Training.

Dogs pull for one of the following reasons:

1. Stress - calm down your dog *before* the walk, see SSCD (p~63)

2. Leash aggression - pay particular attention to Introducing the Short Leash (p~56)

3. Dominance - pay particular attention to becoming the *accepted* Pack leader (p~27)

4. Unreleased energy - forget about *dog walking*, start to exercise your dog more heavily

5. Stimulus aggression (eg squirrel, cat, motorbiker, other dog) - catch up on socializing the dog!! If you have missed that, see the Puppy Development Guide - Puppy 101 (mygermanshepherd.org/go/puppy-development-guide)

6. Fear - don't pay attention to the stimulus yourself, instead distract your dog or turn away - see in detail in the Dog Training Toolkit (mygermanshepherd.org/go/dog-training-toolkit)

In case of reason 1, 2, 3, or 5, in addition the dog suffers a <u>conflict in the Pack</u>, thus like with 3 first focus on becoming your dog's *accepted* Pack leader (p~27).

In case of reason 6, in addition be generally more supportive, help your dog to feel safe - but *don't* speak to or praise your dog in *this* moment, because that would make the incident more memorable, effectively you would *train* your dog to have fear.

For all cases of reason 6, a soft but snug-fit **harness** can help a lot to treat the dog's anxiety. There you have another reason why we shouldn't rule out a harness.

What About a Head Collar?

In recent years, the 'gentle leader' <u>head collar</u> (mygermanshepherd.org/go/head-collar) has become a vastly successful phenomenon - *in sales.* Over 2.5 *million* dog owners have tried the 'gentle leader' head collar - on their dog. It is meant to stop leash pulling, lunging and jumping.

Weirdly, I've never seen *any* dog owner actually using the head collar. Not one. But of those who have tried it, most dog owners seem to be excited about the results.

As <u>dog lovers</u> (see the book title), we are more concerned about whether <u>the dogs</u> are excited too, or only the owners?

For good reason, even the vendor of this particular head collar admits that "it can take long and a lot of effort to desensitize the dog from wearing this collar".

Why? Because the nose loop is so exceptionally irritating for most dogs that even after long and laborious desensitization work many dogs 'refuse' to wear the head collar!

Same tip as always: Try it on yourself. Or, if you don't want to buy one to test it, lick a single oat from your breakfast bag of oats and stick it on your nose, anywhere. Now walk. You'll notice that any item somewhere in front of your eyes is *extremely* irritating. Outright painful to your nerves. Same for dogs!

This is probably best documented with this dog owner's review (amazon.com/review/R2BOKRKM 2QPCV2):

"*He became so frustrated by the collar that he would rub his face on the concrete, claw at the nose strap, and come away bleeding. I returned to desensitizing him to the collar, assuming I had not given him enough time to adjust. I found myself spending more time training him to accept the collar than working on modifying his unwanted behaviors*"

For me personally, I don't need to think twice whether I could make a dog happy with the head collar. Again, if you are in any doubt, the absolutely best test always is to <u>try it on yourself</u>. See if you like the head collar. If you do, surely as dog lover you will then want to give your dog such a head collar. If you don't like it, you may not want to. I don't.

"But it stops the pulling!!!" - Yes, fine. Shooting the dog stops the pulling too. But why choosing the inferior if there is a superior solution?

This of course is to **train** your dog not to pull. Thankfully, you got this Leash Training Guide! So, apply it. It won't get any better. Don't procrastinate.

Save the money of the head collar, and instead get a quality <u>light soft padded genuine leather collar</u> (mygermanshepherd.org/go/bestselling-leather-collar) or maybe the cheap <u>bestselling harness from Puppia</u> (mygermanshepherd.org/go/dog-harness-cheap), whatever you feel your dog will like more.

ID Tag

I firmly believe that when outdoors, *every* dog should wear a collar (or harness), and with an ID tag attached. Personally, I'd even recommend to micro-chip your dog (mygermanshepherd.org/periodical/micro-chipping-your-dog) - but that's not a Leash Training topic, hence only the link in case you are interested (very much worth reading)!

The ID tag should bear the dog's name, your name and telephone number, and a personal note - but <u>not</u> your address (not even the state).

- The dog's name, so that your dog is easier to handle.

- Your name, so that - regardless who gets hold of your dog - the person feels more inclined to call you (it's proven that having a name of someone is a psychological motivator).

- Your *complete* telephone number in international notation! Because, believe it or not, your dog wouldn't be the first dog that - against all odds, and being a total mystery - ends up somewhere abroad, with the collar and tag still attached!

- <u>Not</u> your address, to prevent data privacy issues - and if it only helps to prevent a robbery in your absence...! The address is not needed: If someone has your dog and wants to contact you, they will phone you, not visit you.

- I advise *against* an email address: There are a hundred technical reasons why you may not get to see their message - while they will think you got it! Conversely, if they couldn't reach you on the phone, it is highly likely they will try again later.

- The personal note is a further (great!) psychological motivator. Unless your dog truly needs regular medical attention, the smartest note is this: "Chronically dehydrated, give plenty of water".

Again, it is proven that such a personal note *immensely* impacts on people's motivation to take action - and that's what we want when they have our dog. We want them to care for our dog, and to call us.

The problem with ID tags is that most of them rather easily come off! So, better get a *non-come-off* flat-attaching ID tag (mygermanshepherd.org/go/ dog-collar-tag) from the outset:

There are much posher ones available, I know. But I hope you won't get in that situation where you wish you had chosen the more *practical* ID tag, like the above.

(Yes, I know the photo doesn't reflect the recommendations I just gave, sadly the ID tag vendors haven't read this book. You may want to recommend it to them :-)

Short Leash

With all the chapters above, it is obvious that the **leash** actually takes a backseat in Leash Training. Surprise, surprise!

In terms of leash, most dog owners only know and only have a **short leash** - or a retractable leash. The best retractable leash (mygermanshepherd.org/go/ retractable-leash) can even restrain a stronger dog - but I wouldn't trust the clasp to hold a really strong dog.

Note that the short leash you get should reflect your dog's size and strength, *and* where you can walk your dog:

- If you live in a densely populated area with high traffic etc, or in the woods, then a retractable leash may not be sensible (unless you have the time to solve the resulting puzzles).

- If you have a toy breed or other small dog, then the weight of a robust leather leash alone may exhaust your dog (plus, it would look very odd). In such case a feather-light leash like this top model may be best: mygermanshepherd.org/ go/puppy-leash

- For mid-size to large dogs, the best short leash I know of, based on all feedback to mygermanshepherd.org, is the robust <u>multi-purpose leather teaching lead from Sarah Hodgson</u> (mygermanshepherd.org/go/teaching-lead). It can be used traditionally, hands-free(!), as training aid, as dog parking lot, etc. It is truly multi-purpose. And it's made of genuine leather with reliable hardware, which explains the higher price.

We will use the short leash for <u>SSCD</u> (p~63 - you can do this with a retractable leash too, just keep it short), and whenever we want to keep our dog close by in a highly distracting environment or situation.

For dogs, all outdoor situations are distracting, and in such standard situations we keep the dog *off-leash* <u>once fully leash-trained</u> (or on a long leash, see next).

Long Leash

Unless you can only walk your dog on high traffic roads, I suggest that you consider the short leash (p~51) as last resort, and the **long leash** or **long line** as your standard physical restraint.

The purpose of a long line is to allow our dog to roam freely while we keep ultimate control. This is necessary when we have a puppy, helpful when we train the <u>Recall</u> (p~83), and essential in every environment and situation where we need to prevent a threat or risk to our dog or to the public.

When we need to stop our dog, we *gently* <u>step on</u> the long line, and in the rare case where we need to get our dog back to us and the Recall isn't yet working, we <u>give a gentle tug</u> to indicate that we are still in control regardless.

This case should be rare because, when our dog is on a 50 feet long line we must consciously observe a 50 feet radius around ourselves! No use of the phone, no chatting, no reading. Just observing. Learning from our dog's behavior what (s)he is doing *when* and *where*, so that we can learn about the *why*.

This helps enormously to predict our dog's behavior going forward. Predicting our dog's behavior is a key part of **Behavior Training**: It allows to avoid unnecessary commands (eg "COME here" when there's no risk, no problem, no nada!), and thus it keeps us cool and our dog cool, and we save our commands for when we *really* need them.

Makes all sense, hm?

The <u>best long line</u> is the feather-light 50 feet long line from Sarah Hodgson (mygermanshepherd.org/go/long-line) - no, I am not related to her, and I have no benefit from mentioning two of her products - they are simply the best I know of.

This long line is not just long and light, it also slides well over the ground, which is essential to give the dog the feeling of being free!

Now that we have discussed the <u>Right Equipment</u> (p~31), we can get to the actual Leash Training, hurray! :-)

Introducing the Short Leash

Leash aggression and loads of **leash problems** can be completely avoided by introducing the dog to the leash the *right* way. However, when we get a new dog (and puppy alike), this is what typically happens:

We visit the breeder or shelter, and the dog or puppy we selected earlier is brought to us ... on a leash. After our most excited greeting, and the dog's curious sniffing, the dog is handed over to us and the breeder or shelter leash is being swapped for ... our own leash that we brought with us!

Conversely, this is how *we* introduce a new dog or puppy to the short leash, and you may want to consider to do it similarly:

1. We take a leash with us, wrapped like a present (no fancy paper needed, this is what dogs see: mygermanshepherd.org/periodical/gsd-eye-care)

2. When the dog or puppy is brought to us, we bend down or sit down to greet our new dog. When the greeting and sniffing is done, we get the dog excited about the package ("huuh, look what we have here for you! A preseeeeeent!!" bla bla...)

3. We *slowly* unwrap the package, with loads of excitement and sniffing throughout. We lift the leash from the paper and allow more excited sniffing

4. Then we rotate the dog's collar such that the ring faces down - not at the neck and not in front of the throat but on the outer underside

5. Because next, we *gently and slowly* clip the leash on the collar, at the <u>outer underside</u>! Ie we do everything in a way that the dog can see what we do. And we do all very slowly

6. We continue to demonstrate our excitement about this wonderful present (the short leash)

7. Next, we <u>just stand up</u>, nothing else. Anticipating that we are about to go somewhere, our new dog is likely to 'dance' a bit further away from us, possibly even trying to run away, to lead us where to go

8. But we don't go, we <u>just stand still</u>. The dog will try to see how far (s)he can go with the leash attached, and we give the dog plenty of time to find out. 2 min, 5 min, no problem. We are in training.

9. Once our new dog comes back to us the full length (possibly even circling around us), and visibly has *calmed down*, we <u>make two or three steps</u> - in our chosen direction, not in the direction our dog may have indicated (s)he wants to go

10. Then again, we <u>stand still</u>. And again, the dog will want to experience how far (s)he can go with the leash attached, and we give the dog plenty of time to find out. 2 min, 5 min, no problem. We are in training.

11. We <u>continue step 9 and 10</u> at least 3 more times (10 times if you and the breeder or shelter manager have the time!?)

That's it!

What <u>this introduction</u> to the leash does is:

- it introduces the leash as **something great**, something to be excited about in a positive way *when we have it* for our dog

- it consciously demonstrates to our new dog or puppy that <u>we</u> determine *when* to go, and *where* to go

- it *subconsciously* demonstrates that we only go *anywhere* when our dog is calm

- and it shows our new dog that the leash gives a certain limit as to how far (s)he can get away from us

All this *without* our dog getting the impression that we ourselves limit the dog in any way! This is crucial: We didn't pull back on the leash at any moment. We didn't even take a single step while the leash was tight. We will never do.

If you <u>introduce a dog to the leash *this* way</u>, then there will be **no leash aggression** from the outset. And very little pulling, from the outset. Any pulling will only be playful excitement or fear, no dominance in any way! See again <u>Why Dogs Pull</u> (p~43).

Keep this book for your next dog, try this **leash introduction**, and see what a massive difference this makes for your new dog's overall behavior, not just on the leash. You'll be amazed!

I often hear: "Your books should come with every dog" - and I agree. Most dog owners would do so much better if only they got the right tools from the outset.

However, being realistic: This is not the way your present dog was introduced to the leash, right? So the question is:

Can we re-introduce a dog to the leash the *right* way?

Yes, we can. But to *undo* the earlier introduction of the leash requires a bit more work (of the same as above) than what would otherwise have been required.

Can we use the same leash that our dog already has?

No, the dog couldn't attribute that 'great feeling' to the existing leash (see the first bullet point above) and build new neuronal connections. Not even if we wrap it nicely, because the dog knows the smell. So yes, we will need a new short leash (p~51).

It doesn't actually have to be *new*, but it needs to be new to our dog. A second-hand leash *could* do if the smell doesn't repel, upset, or scare our dog. But how do we know? With a second-hand leash, we cannot know this beforehand.

The Dog Walk

Before the Walk

The next area of leash training many dog owners overlook is the **preparation before the walk**. Clearly, Hollywood actor Ben Affleck missed this too:

We basically continue where our introduction to the short leash ended (p~56). You may or may not know from the Complete House Training Guide (mygermanshepherd.org/go/house-training-guide) that a new dog, and a puppy all the more, need to be walked frequently and *regularly*. For the exact 'dog walk routine' I referred to **this Leash Training**

Guide. Because, for successful Leash Training, at least for the first weeks, <u>the dog walk starts before the walk</u>:

1.   Say 5 to 10 minutes before a regular scheduled walk, we let our dog <u>watch us</u> while we take down the <u>short leash</u> (p~51) from the door handle, we *slowly* walk to our dog, and we *gently* attach the leash to the dog's <u>collar</u> (p~33) or <u>harness</u> (p~39).

2.   Now we let our dog walk around in the house with the leash attached, while the end of the leash hangs loose - ie don't clip the second carabiner into the D-ring at the end of the lead, if it has one, like the superior teaching lead has (p~51).

3.   This is how the dog gets used to something hanging *loose* off its neck (or withers), and will not make a fuzz out of it later during the walk - unless we were suddenly starting to pull the leash tight, which we won't.

4.   Say 2 minutes before the regular scheduled walk, we pick up the end of the lead and do some <u>SSCD</u> inside the house. This is the next chapter.

SSCD

SSCD is the next step of **preparation before the walk**. SSCD stands for <u>S</u>tart - <u>S</u>top - <u>C</u>hange <u>D</u>irection. SSCD has many purposes, and for Leash Training its key purpose is:

- to get our dog to <u>match our movements</u>, and

- to <u>calm down</u> entirely before we even go outside!

SSCD is highly effective and very simple. A 5-year old can do it. So, don't over-complicate it. It works like this:

- Attach the <u>short leash</u> (p~51) to your dog's <u>collar</u> (p~33) or <u>harness</u> (p~39)

- **Start** to walk slowly in one direction

- **Stop** when you want, or when your dog pulls (in any direction)

- **Change Direction**

Continue to **Start, Stop,** and **Change Direction**. That's it! I said, it's very simple. But incredibly effective!

Repeat **SSCD** for a few minutes before the regular scheduled walk, or until your dog is totally calm: Always start to walk slowly in one direction, then stop whenever you want or when your dog pulls (anywhere), and then turn to change direction.

You will notice that your dog will quickly learn to match your movements ("heel") very well, and (s)he will be so much calmer when you actually go for the walk! Because **SSCD** is significantly *calming* for a dog. Unless of course, we are stressed ourselves (remember, dogs are energy recipients, p~19 - this becomes very clear with the Dog Training Toolkit).

If despite this hopefully clear description you'd prefer to actually *see* how a top professional dog trainer makes use of SSCD, then Dan Abdelnoor (Doggy Dan) is the best to learn from: His extensive online video library of *live* dog training situations with clients (mygermanshepherd.org/go/online-dog-trainer) shows exactly how to perform SSCD *right* (and any other dog training matter). It's not completely free but peanuts compared to a local dog trainer.

Going through the Door

After 1) our dog has been <u>walking around the house with the leash attached</u> (p~61), and 2) we have done some <u>SSCD</u> (p~63) and we are happy with our dog matching our movements and being calm, next we lead the dog to the main door and open it.

Regardless of our chosen potty routine (as described in the Complete House Training Guide), for Leash Training too we will require our dog to stay *behind us* when we are going through the door for the walk.

If our dog tries to get around our legs to go out first, we close the door and do some more <u>SSCD</u> (p~63). We will only go out through the main door once our dog calmly stays *behind us*.

Training to HEEL During Leash Walking

After 1) our dog has been walking around the house with the leash attached (p~61), and 2) we have done some SSCD (p~63) and we are happy with our dog matching our movements and being calm, and 3) our dog calmly stays *behind us* when we are going through the door (p~65), only *now* we go outside and start the Leash Walk, yeah!

It is those dog owners (and trainers!) who miss all the **preparation before the walk** who then struggle with leash-pulling, lunging, jumping, or even their dog running off. Or, who swear on the head collar (p~45) despite their dog suffering from it.

Just to be sure: Leash walk means we use the short leash (p~51). And during every leash walk we train a bit of heeling - but no more than a bit! Most dog owners I've seen in the streets (and even in the woods) are either being pulled by their dog(!) - or are making their dog heel *all the time*.

Why?? Why does the poor dog have to heel all the time?

Both is wrong. Because as dog lovers:

- we want a *calm* dog
- who *enjoys* the walk

- the walk gives the dog loads of *distraction* from the daily boredom

- the walk gives the dog the freedom to exercise its entire body

- but the walk also trains the dog to heel <u>when needed</u>

When is Heeling Needed?

Heeling is needed:

- when we pass strangers, children, or animals - to make *them* feel at ease
- when we come to precarious terrain
- when we are near streets with high traffic

But when there's nothing nearby that warrants to worry about, then why make the dog heel? Why deny our dog to *enjoy* the walk and to get loads of distraction from the daily boredom, as well as healthy all-round exercise?

As <u>dog lovers</u> we don't. Maybe this is a good point to re-read the <u>Mindset</u> (p~19).

When, Where, and How to Train Heeling

Initially, we let our dog get to the designated potty place as fast as (s)he wants (within reason).

<u>After</u> relieving, we exercise our dog, and during the exercise we embed some heel training.

We start at a place with as few distractions as possible, ideally where we are alone with our dog (no other people, no other animals, no traffic). A quiet road, a park, the woods, all is good.

Now we get our dog's attention (I call out the dog's name). If you've done all the <u>indoor dog walk preparation</u> described earlier (p~61), your dog will be *very calm and receptive* for what you say and do. So (s)he will stop walking and look up at you to detect what you could possibly want.

Since *we* <u>behavior-train</u> our dogs (mygermanshep herd.org/periodical/advanced-dog-training-behavior -training), I now do the following, and you may want to do it similarly:

1. I demonstratively tap my left thigh twice and say HEEL (you can use the right thigh too)

I use the left thigh on right-hand traffic roads because I would walk on the side of the oncoming traffic, and the dog must be on the other side of me - all for safety.

2. If the dog doesn't come close to my indicated leg, I <u>wait</u> a few seconds and then I <u>repeat</u> both the tapping and the vocal cue (we are in training, so repeating a cue is perfectly acceptable)

Note that I don't raise my voice or anything - one of the reasons why I <u>wait</u> a few seconds before I repeat the cue: I breathe to consciously stay calm. Then I calmly repeat both the tapping and the vocal cue.

3. I repeat 2) until successful (while standing still). I don't do anything else, we are in training.

4. When the dog settles close to my indicated leg, I *bend down* to reward with some affection *and* praise (WELL DONE)

5. *Now* I start to walk, and the dog will definitely walk with me - but (s)he must keep close to my indicated leg. If (s)he doesn't walk close to my indicated leg, I say STOP and stop walking. I start over again at 1) above.

—————————————

That's it! You see it's really *easy* if you do it <u>right</u> and you are consistent. And it works great!

But don't forget to <u>release</u> your dog after a bit of heeling - for a dog, lengthy heeling is *stressful* because it comes in addition to all the distracting stimuli in the outdoor environment.

So, after say a minute or two (max) of perfect heeling, I say STOP and stop walking, and the dog will definitely stop too. I look down, demonstratively *smile* (with closed mouth), and then bend down to reward with some affection *and* praise (WELL DONE). Then I straighten up and - *while* I show the dedicated visual cue (I use a swift outwards and upwards movement with my hand) - I say RELEASE!

Since now I will no longer stop when the dog leaves the side of my leg, the dog quickly learns that the final cue (RELEASE) means that (s)he's free to stroll around where (s)he wants - and in this case, what (s)he can reach while on-leash (because we are in Training to Heel During Leash Walking, p~66).

Final notes:

- Important is that we then practice the **on-leash heel training** in ever more distracting environments and situations. So, after say 10 or 15 min (minimum), I will again confine the dog to some heel training - with a minor distraction (say a person in the distance). Then later the next session, while say a dog is in the distance. Then while a dog is close by, etc etc.

- With each new level of distraction, where our dog *doesn't* comply, we <u>return to the prior level of difficulty</u> that the dog had mastered successfully earlier on, and we proceed as shown above (step 1 to 5).

- With a **puppy**, training sessions must be <u>much shorter</u> (say 10 seconds of heeling), and we will be <u>more lenient</u> (no perfect heeling required from a puppy).

Introducing the Long Leash

Surprisingly *many* dog owners have neither seen nor heard of a 'long leash' or 'long line' - and thus never used one. This is surprising, because a long line is <u>so helpful</u> in Leash Training!

This is how *we* introduce a new dog or puppy to the <u>long leash</u> (p~54), and you may want to consider to do it similarly:

1. Again, wrapped like a present (no fancy paper needed - remember, <u>this is what dogs see</u>: my germanshepherd.org/periodical/gsd-eye-care), we take the long line with us on a walk

2. When we've reached some deserted open space, we say or signal STOP and stop walking. We look down, demonstratively smile (with closed mouth), and then <u>bend down or sit down</u> and get the dog excited about the package ("huuh, look what we have here for you! A preseeeeeent!!" bla bla...)

3. We *slowly* unwrap the package, with loads of excitement and sniffing throughout

4. We lift the long leash from the paper and allow more excited sniffing

5. Then we detach the short leash from the collar, and *gently and slowly* clip on the new long leash (remember, always on the *outer underside*, not at the neck or in front of the throat)

6. We continue to demonstrate our excitement about this wonderful present (the long line) - it really is wonderful, it gives freedom, both of us!

7. Next, we <u>just stand up</u>, nothing else. By now our dog has long learned that when we straighten up it doesn't mean (s)he can run away - the dog will *stay* and look what we do next

8. Now we demonstratively look down at the long leash, and a second later we give the release cue (I use a swift outwards and upwards movement with my hand while I say RELEASE) - and then the dog will spurt away

Note that while in training, combining a visual with a vocal cue makes sense. Later, we may often just want to give the visual cue, because it is enough.

9. Since the long line is ... well ... *long* (50 feet if you get the right one, p~54), it is unlikely that it tightens anytime soon. Speaking of it: <u>long line time is free time</u>, so we will rather walk after the dog if (s)he needs more line (freedom), we don't pull back! - When needed for safety, or at end, we gently step on it (see later, <u>Switching Back to Short Leash</u>, p~95).

What this *theater performance* of <u>introducing the long leash</u> does: Our dog or puppy now associates the long leash with **something great** (imminent <u>free time</u>), and we can use this for a further leash training detail (see next).

Switching from Short to Long Leash

Going forward, whenever we go on a walk where we know we will reach some safe open space, we take the <u>long leash</u> with us (p~54) - but we only switch from short to long leash when during the <u>heeling sessions</u> (p~69) our dog heeled well (an adult dog perfectly well, a puppy reasonably well).

This further trains our dog the difference between matching our movements (heeling) and the freedom to roam around. Indeed, this *difference* must be made very clear, because it further motivates the dog to heel very well <u>when we require it</u> (which shouldn't be that often, see <u>When is Heeling Needed</u>, p~68): The dog learns that close heeling is a prerequisite to get free time. A wonderful motivation for a dog!

When we want to switch from short to long leash:

- We say STOP and stop walking. We look down and demonstratively smile (with closed mouth) at the long line and then at our dog, and then we <u>bend down</u> to switch the leash

- Now simply repeat all from step 5 above (see <u>Introducing the Long Leash</u>, p~73).

Note that obviously you don't need to say STOP when you stop walking while your dog is next to you. Only when our dog is slightly ahead (ie when heeling is not needed) I give the vocal cue too, so that the leash won't tighten up when I stop.

If you consider a <u>tight leash</u> as a *setback* for your Leash Training, your progress with Leash Training will be fastest!

Training the STAY Command

Our way of <u>Introducing the Long Leash</u> (p~73) allows us a further training detail that we need later for our Leash Training: the STAY command.

When our dog is on the <u>long line</u> (p~54) and has had some time to explore the vicinity, we must catch a *suitable* moment to train the STAY command. Suitable moments are:

- when our dog is <u>coming back</u> to us - which usually happens every so often, even when dogs are playing with each other

- when our dog is <u>looking</u> at us - even from a distance

- when our dog '<u>freezes</u>' - which often happens when the dog has encountered someone or something and is unsure what to do.

When you catch any of these moments, you can say or signal your dog to STAY. I myself use the index finger in a swift downwards movement until it points horizontally towards the dog. I keep my finger in this position for a moment to see if the dog stops walking. If not, I <u>repeat</u> the cue while I say STAY.

After two failed attempts I would stop and defer the training to later. Because: Some dogs can be quite stubborn during training. It doesn't help an inch to press it. I just defer to later. That's why it's called **training**.

The final **result** of training is that the dog will follow our cues <u>out of routine</u> (without much thinking). This *routine* cannot be established when you press for success!

When upon our visual and/or vocal cue the dog stops walking, the goal for the STAY command is achieved, great! But what next? This is where most dog trainers and owners *mess up* the STAY training, because they don't have a clear idea what the STAY is for. There are three possible reasons for the STAY:

1. We want the dog to stop walking so that we can catch up to put the dog on the lead

2. We want the dog to stop walking *further* away from us, and instead COME back to us

3. We want the dog to stop walking only to stand still so that (s)he won't get into danger (a nearby road or whatever)

Note that you cannot start training the STAY command if your goal is 1) - Why should your dog want to stand still and wait for you to be put on-leash? No, (s)he won't! That's the dog owners you can see walking to their dog, and when they come close, their dog escapes, again and again. Funny to watch them. :-)

If you train your dog to *expect* to be put on-leash after a STAY, your dog will not comply with the STAY for long! *You* wouldn't either, and I wouldn't either.

Note that likewise, you cannot start training the STAY command if your goal is 2) - If you mix the STAY with the COME, you water down both!

Later, when your dog has learned to *routinely* comply with the STAY in a variety of challenging situations, *then* you can use the STAY for 1) and 2) as well. But initially, you must **start training** the STAY with situation 3) in mind. 3) only!

So: When upon our visual and/or vocal cue the dog stops walking, we slowly and calmly <u>walk to</u> our dog, without further ado. When we reach the dog, we *don't* put our dog on-leash, we don't talk, we don't touch, and we don't look. We let **our behavior** speak for itself: When we give the cue, then to STAY is the normal thing to do, it is what we expect, and our dog does not learn to expect that (s)he will then be put on-leash or anything.

Instead, we simply walk past our dog, thus that <u>the dog learns from our behavior</u> that now (s)he may continue to roam around.

IF we feel we need to calm down our dog, we would then simply perform the **Collar Freeze**: We *gently* take hold of the collar, on the outer underside (not at the neck or throat), and then <u>we freeze</u>. We transmit our low energy to our dog - remember, dogs are energy recipients (p~19), so you *must* be calm yourself.

If executed right, dogs *love* the Collar Freeze because dogs prefer to be calm and safe and close to their Pack, and they adapt to their Pack leader's state of mind - see The Mindset (p~19) and Something Else We Need (p~27).

We perform the Collar Freeze for a minute or until the dog is calm - *if (s)he wasn't before*. And then we RELEASE the dog, so that (s)he can continue to roam freely - while still on the long line (we are training the STAY command!).

This is the only way to train the STAY command successfully, such that later we can widen its scope and it will always work: We then train the STAY command in ever more demanding situations. Eg:

- next we take a few steps backwards while our dog has to STAY

- then we turn around

- then we walk away

- then we run away

- then we practice all this again but with people close by who are *distracting* our dog

- etc

Each time our dog has to calmly remain on the spot, despite what we are doing after signaling STAY, and despite how much our dog gets distracted by the environment or situation.

This is the quickest way to successfully train your dog the STAY command, regardless of the environment and situation.

Training the RECALL

Now we are ready for the real deal of **Leash Training**: the **Recall**!

Recall means getting our dog to COME when called. It is the ultimate goal of leash training, and the proud of every dog owner. Little is more embarassing (and annoying) than having to call your dog so loud and often that everyone within a mile is turning their head - just not your dog! Have you seen this with others? I have. So many times.

Despite its significance, the **Recall** seems to remain the most challenging training objective even for long time dog owners - and trainers! But thankfully, you now have this one-of-a-kind Leash Training Guide, oh yeah! :-)

Outdoors, the **Recall** certainly is the most crucial dog command - if you see it as a command. I don't, I see it as a motivator.

Why?

Watch the secret (mygermanshepherd.org/go/the-secret) ... or just see the next chapter ;-)

The Secret to a Successful Recall

The Recall is a <u>motivator</u> because, whenever we call our dog to us, we *must* have a GREAT experience for our dog - or else the Recall will soon no longer work reliably!

<u>Calling our dog</u> means that we have something GREAT for the dog (indoors or outdoors)

What??

Yes! Calling our dog does <u>not</u> mean that we give a *command* and the dog *has* to come, or (s)he'll face some form of *enforcement*. I can frankly tell you, if you see the Recall that way, you will never get a successful Recall in tempting outdoor situations - ie when you need it most, and if for safety alone.

So let me repeat the secret, because it is crucially important: Whenever you call your dog to you, you *must* make sure that you have a GREAT experience for your dog when (s)he's coming!

As great experience I usually offer 'grade 1' <u>praise</u> combined with 'grade 1' <u>affection</u>, or a favorite toy or play or a real-life reward (for details on all <u>Reward Types</u> see the <u>Dog Training Toolkit</u>: mygermanshepherd.org/go/dog-training-toolkit).

That was part *one* of the secret, now comes part two:

When we *don't* have something GREAT for our dog, and likewise when we have a potentially *negative* experience awaiting, then we must walk to the dog!

Examples: To put on the lead ("Oh, she's tying me at the *neck* again!!"), or to perform the Collar Freeze ("Uuh, why is he coming so close?"), or to provide Mouth Care ("What does she want with this thing in my mouth?!").

When to call your dog, and when to walk to your dog - this is one of the most fundamental dog training skills - and it requires practice!

But, watching most dog owners (and trainers!), I realize that this skill is still a secret.

Despite teaching others this, I sometimes notice that I myself *just* made an error: While the principle above sounds obvious and easy, it does take a lot of practice to get used to it - and even then you'll sometimes overlook it!

Maybe this is because, we humans are 'socially programmed' the opposite way: When we have potentially bad news, we will rarely walk to the person and deliver it (rather we wait and hope someone else might do it). And when we have a present, we don't call the person to us to collect it, rather we walk to the person to deliver it (before someone else does).

With canines, we must adapt to the exact opposite - for both situations!

You will need to continually practice this - I have to do too. If you have a family, it's easier because one of you might notice the other's mistake. Make a game out of it: Whenever one catches a family member doing it wrong, a chore is due. ;-)

It is the dog owners who *don't* follow this simple advice who have a problem to <u>recall</u> their dog from something attractive while outdoors. It really does all start with the simple <u>calling our dog</u> indoors, and then providing a GREAT experience. Every time.

Think from your dog's point of view: Why should an animal(!) run towards you when <u>you</u> want it, if that animal (namely your dog) hasn't learned from prior experience that you have something absolutely amazing for him/her!?

It's already hard to get our children or partner to run towards us when *we* want it, isn't it? So why should we expect from an animal (no matter how much domesticated) that it does so?

Well, we *can* actually achieve this with domesticated dogs, because dogs love to *please us* (it has been bred into them for thousands of years) - but only if we are the _accepted_ Pack leader (p~27). Until then, we will have to give our dog a GREAT reason to COME when _we_ want that. Every time.

Even after we have established ourselves as _accepted_ Pack leader, we should sporadically provide a random great reward when our dog is coming when called, because that helps to reinforce the dog's memory that coming to us may offer a GREAT experience.

Total Recall

Now, to keep this chapter short, let's make a list of the <u>key points for a successful Recall</u> - or Total Recall. :-)

1. <u>Introduce</u> the (new) leash the right way (p~51) and start with our <u>Leash Training</u> (p~56) ideally immediately the day after you get your dog or puppy. There is no 'too young' or 'too early'. Perform all Leash Training stages as described, since Leash Training is at the heart of the Recall.

2. From the outset, only give a reward for <u>behavior you desire</u> (not eg for "looking so cute!" or because you are "having a great day" or whatever), and only when you've called your dog or puppy <u>to you</u>. Don't let weeks or even months pass by while you give rewards without having called your dog, or where you did call your dog but then provided a mediocre experience.

3. Train yourself to *ignore* your dog whenever (s)he comes to you to *collect* a reward without being called. This may appear 'harsh' to you but it is exactly how dogs learn to behave in their dog pack too!

4. Be clear about what you want from your dog, be confident (p~24), and don't confuse your dog with inconsistency.

5. Before each meal, always perform Gesture Eating (mygermanshepherd.org/periodical/dog-meals-meal-times-and-feeding-routine). This is the key success factor to establish yourself as *accepted* Pack leader!

6. Only ever give your dog a meal, treat, toy, pat, cuddle or other affection when you have called your dog to you (we had that? Good that you remember, it is essential!)

7. When you call your dog to you, and your dog doesn't *immediately* shoot towards you but then comes a bit later, ignore your dog (see 3) - like (s)he just *decided* to ignore you too, namely to demonstrate his/her dominance in the Pack structure, as considered by your dog.

In other words: Give your dog only *one* chance to come when called, and then to get the Reward you intended to give - which should always be something very worthwhile.

8. If your dog decides not to make use of that *one* chance, then within a few times/days only (s)he will have completely understood that the chance is lost with the first call. Because thereafter (s)he is being *ignored* - like your dog just ignored you too, and like (s)he was ignored in the dog pack already as a puppy!

Domesticated dogs don't like to be ignored by humans, they have been bred to *thrive* on human attention. They *need* it - almost as much as food and water! If you don't believe this, go and visit a few shelters to see how the dogs without human interaction 'go nuts' (despite food and water), while the dogs who are being looked after once a while, stay reasonably sane (despite being locked up).

9. Don't say anything when your dog just didn't come when called (like "No, you just ignored me, now I ignore you", or "This is part of your training, you see, you better come when I call you", or similar bullshit) - NO. Don't even look at your dog, no matter how begging or cute (s)he now looks at you.

10. *Never* call your dog away from <u>food, water, or potty time</u>!

11. Find out what your dog LOVES (mygerm anshepherd.org/periodical/german-shepherd-top-treats). Initially, motivate your dog to come immediately when called by *randomly* giving just that. Not every time (then it would lose its high attraction), but sometimes.

12. Don't focus on food treats - and *randomize* all rewards given.

13. Never use punishment (wannabe-intellectuals like to call it 'negative reinforcement', but the term is nonsense, see here why: bit.ly/1cjLOdy). So, never threaten your dog with a harsh voice, raised arm, actions, or longer-lasting withdrawal of attention and affection, or food, water, potty-going, or similar.

Only when we have mastered all of the above, including all stages of Leash Training (p~56), we start to practice the **Recall**. This is done outdoors:

14. First, go to a place where you are alone with your dog, and after 2 or 3 minutes of SSCD (p~63) with the short leash (p~51), switch to the long leash (p~76)

15. Say GO, RELEASE, AWAY (or whatever cue you use to release your dog in order to be free to do what (s)he wants), and let your dog run around <u>as (s)he pleases</u>. Ensure that the <u>long line</u> (p~54) always remains loose (ie in this case, *go after* your dog if (s)he needs more than the 50 feet)

16. Then after say 10 minutes free time, <u>call your dog once</u> (but make sure (s)he heard you) and while doing so even *walk away*, indicating you are 'leaving'.

17. With all the inhouse training before (p~61), your dog should now immediately speed towards you - *whether or not* you show a food treat, so <u>don't</u> show a food treat!

If your dog doesn't immediately speed towards you, no problem, <u>show no grudge</u>: You have just tried your *first* Recall, practice the same entire routine more often now.

18. Essential (often forgotten): Once the **Recall** is always successful in a place where you are alone with your dog, practice the Recall under increasingly more distracting conditions: People nearby, other dogs nearby, a lonely large piece of meat at a barbecue, or any other highly attractive distraction.

19. Only when you are happy with your dog following your call *every time* while on the <u>long line</u> (mygermanshepherd.org/go/long-line), then you can take off the long line and <u>re-start</u> all your training (initially in a place where you are alone with your dog)

20. Just remember not to overdo it: The *less* you call your dog (the less restrictive and/or dominant you are, really) the more impact it will have *when* you do it!

When you adopt all the above **20 points**, your Recall will become nearly 100% successful - a **Total Recall** so to say. You will then find yourself seeking out the vicinity of other dog owners, just to impress them - I did. ;-)

If you find 20 *written* points slightly overwhelming, remember that the <u>*professional* dog trainer Doggy Dan</u> has *live* dog training videos on every subject matter, including the Recall (mygermanshepherd.org/go/ online-dog-trainer).

While I agree that *seeing and hearing* how to train your dog is extremely helpful, I would argue that videos nicely complement but cannot substitute the written insight that we get from good books.

Regardless how you learn best: Little is more rewarding for us dog owners than calling our dog *once*, and the dog is speeding towards us like a happy bird in an upwind. :-)

Indeed, a reliable Recall makes a vast difference to the quality of life - both for your dog and for yourself!

Switching Back to Short Leash

This is another important area to consider, and it applies to two situations:

- When you want to switch back from <u>long leash</u> (p~54) to <u>short leash</u> (p~51)

- When you want to put on the short leash after your dog was entirely off-leash

Both situations your dog may not like at all! Obviously dogs prefer to be *free* over being restricted by the short leash. But now that you know <u>The Secret</u> (p~84) to a <u>Total Recall</u> (p~88), the question is:

How do we get our dog back on the short leash, without calling our dog to us and then providing this *negative* experience of the short leash? And, without running after our dog either!

The only solution I know of is the <u>STAY command</u> in the way described before (p~78). And that's why initially we may only <u>switch to the long line</u> (p~76) in a place where we are alone with our dog, and when we have enough time: The first five times or so of <u>training the STAY command</u> (p~78), we *must* have goal 3) - as explained in the linked chapter (ie that our dog merely <u>stands still</u> and waits for us to catch up, without us doing anything then).

In each such training session, when we have practiced this say five times, the *final* time we can then end the training session by giving loads of affection and praise, and then *gently* putting our dog back on the short leash (p~51), and then even giving more affection and praise. We 'sandwich' the mustard in a large bun (to make the 'mustard' unnoticeable).

This way, the mental connection the dog will remember is: "I STAYED and got lots of affection and praise". <u>Not</u>: "I STAYED and was put on-leash!". This is essential!

But note that we don't want to reward *each* STAY, because we want our dog to develop STAY as <u>routine behavior</u>. We want our dog to build the mental connection: "When I see or hear the cue to STAY, I'll do just that, for my Pack leader to catch up, then I am free to run further".

The Leash-Free Dog

Many councils or communities have established strict leash laws (bylaws). And I can understand why: Too many dog owners don't perform proper leash training, and their off-leash dog scares away passers-by. But this Leash Training Guide documents that it doesn't have to be like that.

When I walk the dogs in a 'leash-law zone', I demonstratively *don't* care about the signs, confident that "every law is only there for those who need it to behave" (that's how I grew up). I know I do behave without the leash law, and the dogs behave too. Hence I don't care about signs.

Sure, I've met those passers-by who cared a LOT, to whom laws and bylaws mean everything (because *they* need them). And some of those passers-by were outright 'aggressive' (to the extent they dared, facing two grown German Shepherds led by a man): "You know you have to have your dogs on-leash!!!"

The assumptions of such well-educated passers-by aside (that I *know*, and that the dogs are *mine*), I then calmly reply: "What dogs? As you see, I am walking here with the two best-behaved friends you can imagine".

If the passer-by looks convinced, I leave it at that. If not, I typically add: "There may come the time when you are in need of my two friends to protect you, and you can be sure they will be there for you *instantly* - unless of course you required them to be *leashed*".

While this usually takes the person a few moments to sink in, I've never had a complaint thereafter from the same person.

Anyway, with regards to the subsequent chapters, at least where you *may* walk your dog off-leash, why not do it? Why deny your dog to *enjoy* the walk and to get loads of distraction from the daily boredom, as well as healthy all-round exercise?

Plus, only when you actually walk your dog *off-leash*, you can fully complete Leash Training, and get confidence about your dog's reliability with STAY, COME, and HEEL - because all these are much more demanding for a dog that physically is free to go anywhere (ie not tied to a leash).

How to UNLEASH a Dog Using SSCD and Long Leash

Now that our dog has learned to <u>match our movements</u> (see SSCD, p~63), and to <u>stay behind us</u> when we require it (see Going through the Door, p~65), and to <u>heel during our dog walk</u> when we require it (see Training to Heel During Leash Walking, p~66), the dog will be *very* receptive to **our behavior**, without the need for us to give many commands at all!

Experience has shown that <u>behavior-trained dogs</u> (mygermanshepherd.org/periodical/advanced-dog-training-behavior-training) pretty much behave the same way whether on-leash or off-leash, and whether under our surveillance or alone at home (see House Training Dogs to Behave Well: mygerm anshepherd.org/go/house-training-guide). This is a difference like night and day to <u>obedience-trained dogs</u> (mygermanshepherd.org/periodical/obedience -training-pros-and-cons).

We really only need to make use of <u>SSCD</u> (p~63) and the <u>Long Leash</u> (p~54) to train our dog to behave equally well when UNLEASHED:

1. To prepare our dog for an UNLEASHED dog walk, we start like always with <u>SSCD</u> *inside* the house and <u>we keep our dog behind us</u> (p~65) before we even go out

2. Now, depending on your neighborhood, it may be safe to put your dog on the <u>long leash</u> (p~54) right from the start, or it may be safer to first use the <u>short leash</u> (p~51) until you reach a place where you are alone with your dog, and then to <u>switch the short leash for the long leash</u> (p~76)

3. In any case, we start the UNLEASHED-Training with some further <u>SSCD</u> (p~63), now *outside*, while the <u>long line</u> (p~54) is attached to our dog - for safety reasons, because we do not necessarily have to have achieved a reliable <u>Recall</u> yet (p~83)

4. This is much more demanding for the dog, but if you've done all the prior training as described, your dog will now again <u>match your movements</u> *without* a physical restraint! The long line is just lying somewhere on the ground, and your dog is pulling it behind - but if you got the right one (mygermanshep herd.org/go/long-line), it's feather-light, almost unnoticeable to the dog

5. If your dog *doesn't* match your movements well, then don't take off the long line today, instead do more indoors <u>SSCD</u> (p~63) and <u>Training to Heel During Leash Walking</u> (p~66), and revisit your <u>Feeding Routine</u> (p~30) to ensure you are the *accepted* Pack leader!

6. Conversely, when your dog matches your movements well for a couple of minutes, despite now being outside (which is always distracting for a dog) and without physical restraint - and if the Recall (p~84) works reliably(?!) - then you can take off the long line as well, and RELEASE your dog. Which means that (s)he's free to stroll around where (s)he wants - and in this case it means: *anywhere*, because the dog is now off-leash.

Therefore, I only UNLEASH the dog from the long line as well when, based on the dog's and my own behavior, I am confident that I can instantly:

- make the dog STAY (p~78) where (s)he currently is

- or COME back to me (p~83) when I have *something great* for the dog (remember this?)

- or HEEL next to my leg (p~69)

Obviously this is for safety reasons: It must not happen that say a roaring motorbike or car, a squirrel, cat or other dog, a cyclist, skateboarder or whatever could motivate the dog to run after it.

There you see why I mentioned in the beginning that, in addition to having the right Mindset (p~19), and being the *accepted* Pack leader (p~27), our dog must have been well **socialized** (normally as a puppy, hence fully covered in the Puppy Deve-

<u>lopment Guide - Puppy 101</u>: mygermanshepherd. org/go/puppy-development-guide).

If <u>all three</u> is a given, then we can even UNLEASH our dog say on busy Oxford Street in London, in Chinatown in New York City, on Colaba Causeway in Mumbai, or in midst any other ueber-hectic crowded place.

But before you do that, see in the next chapter how to train your dog to <u>heel while unleashed</u>.

How to Get an UNLEASHED Dog Heel

This actually is *less* demanding than a reliable <u>Recall</u> (p~83), because our dog is close to us anyway: A dog hesitates more to leave the Pack leader the first five meters than another 5 meters in the distance.

To get an UNLEASHED dog heel, we start the training when we *just* took off the leash. Later, we can even Recall our dog to then <u>heel unleashed</u> for the next 50 meters or so. But initially, it's much easier to train the dog to heel when we *just* took off the short leash:

1. Again, first we start with <u>SSCD</u> (p~63) *inside* the house and <u>we keep our dog behind us</u> (p~65) before we even go out.

2. Then, with the dog on the <u>short leash</u> (p~51), again initially we seek out a place where we are alone with our dog. There, we do some <u>further SSCD</u> (say 2 min, or until the dog matches our movements and is totally calm).

3. Next, we take off the short leash, say and/or signal HEEL, and start to walk slowly - exactly like with the <u>on-leash heel training</u> (see step 1 to 5 and the supporting notes, p~69)

Since the dog *could* now run away, again first I want to be confident that the <u>Recall</u> (p~83) works reliably, before I would UNLEASH the dog (as there is no <u>long line</u> involved now).

As always, once the training result in the deserted place is satisfying, we continue the training with <u>increasing distractions</u>, eg:

- a person in the distance, then close by

- then a dog in the distance, then close by

- then near some light traffic, then near some heavy traffic

- then screaming children on a playground in the distance, then close by

- finally, in the distance anything you know to be upsetting to your dog.

Note: Not to be mean and upset the dog(!), just to check how reliable your dog's response is.

With each new level of distraction where the dog *doesn't* comply (here with UNLEASHED heeling), we <u>return to the prior level of difficulty</u> that the dog had mastered successfully earlier on (exactly as shown with step 1 to 5 in <u>on-leash heel training</u>, p~69).

Remember that with a **puppy**, training sessions must be <u>much shorter</u> than with an adult dog. I'd say, 10 seconds of unleashed heeling is plenty for a pup of 3 months of age. And I would only entirely UNLEASH a seemingly *mature* puppy; a younger pup I'd only give the *impression* of unleashed heeling (while being on the long line, p~54). Also, we will of course be <u>more lenient</u> (no perfect heeling required from a puppy).

Getting Home

Like with <u>leaving the house</u> for a dog walk (p~65), we also follow a certain routine when we get back home, because this significantly improves overall leash training success:

1. No matter how much our dog loves to storm back inside the house (some dogs do), again the dog owner must be the first to go through the door! If needed, we block the entry with our legs.

2. Once inside, we *gently and slowly* take off the leash (if the vicinity of your house is safe, of course you can take off the leash long before reaching home)

3. Straight away, we give some <u>affection and praise</u>

4. Now that we have the dog's attention, we demonstratively hang the leash over the door handle (like where we demonstratively took it from <u>before the walk</u>, p~61)

5. Again, this helps the dog to build the mental connection: Great experience - Leash - Door - Walk

6. Only now we RELEASE the dog to walk around in the house as (s)he pleases (I say RELEASE or OFF YOU GO)

Note that *we* do <u>not</u> crate our dogs (as in 'lock away'), for *why* see <u>House Training Dogs to Behave Well</u> (mygermanshepherd.org/go/house-training-gui de).

──────────────

This concludes the Leash Training Guide, and how to get From On-Leash To Off-Leash - while staying calm and relaxed, and having a more relaxed dog too.

I would strongly recommend that you start with your *new* Leash Training right now. Go through each chapter, practice, and you'll experience: Our **Behavior Training** approach is so much FUN, for both of you!

What next?

If you have an idea how to improve this **Leash Training Guide**, please let me know:

support@mygermanshepherd.org - Thanks!

If instead or in addition you'd like to post a public review for this book, then I will definitely appreciate your review on your favorite social media or bookstore platform.

~~~

Connect with Tim Carter:
https://twitter.com/mygsdorg
http://mygermanshepherd.org/comments/feed/
https://smashwords.com/interview/TimCarter
https://www.goodreads.com/TimCarter
Questions only on the website (a page where it fits the content): http://mygermanshepherd.org

More Books by the Same Author

Puppy Development Guide - Puppy 101: *The Secrets to Puppy Training Without Force, Fear, and Fuss* (mygermanshepherd.org/go/books)

- "Best Training Book I have ever read"

- "Puppy must-have!"

- "Easy to read even experienced dog owners can get something from this book"

House Training Dogs *to Behave Well in a High Value Home* (mygermanshepherd.org/go/books)

House Training is so much more than house-breaking: It is everything to get your dog to behave well in the house while having free run of the house while you are away!

- "Wonderful book/guide, very simple to use methods, the results are phenomenal"

- "Hugely informative, there is so much stuff in here that I didn't know, and it has already helped me with my four month old puppy. House-training and housebreaking are truly very different things"

- "Excellent Guide!! Lots of great ideas and not too technical. Tim writes with the DOG in mind with emphasis on not over-thinking, over-correcting or over-training. I have used many of his methods and suggestions successfully"

- "I was amazed how much I thought I knew but really failed in my conception of family life with a GSD. The information was spot on. The book after reading it twice is a real eye opener and a MUST for dog owners"

The World's Only DOG TRAINING TOOLKIT (mygermanshepherd.org/go/books)

Don't use Force, Don't use Fear, Don't Yell and Don't Shriek. Forget 'training collars' and 'treat training'. Forget Obedience Training. - **Why use *Commands* when we can use *Tools*?**

The Dog Training Toolkit revolutionizes dog training all across the globe: The *gentle* dog training approach that works even with the most difficult rescue dogs.

- "The greatest invention since the emergence of dogs"

- "Excellent. I have tried many of the tools that Tim provides with so much success. I've had several dogs in my lifetime but have the best relationship with my GSD than with any other dog ever"

- "Great insight!"

- "This book is the most comprehensive one I have seen on training your pup/dog"

- "I've had dogs for quite a long time, both rescue and from a puppy. They've all presented unique challenges in their training and I've had to cope with it by myself. With this book you are no longer alone. It covers everything you can think of and more. I wish that this book had been available years ago when I bought my first dog from the shelter, or when I first got a puppy."

The Shorties:

mygermanshepherd.org/go/books

Not to forget!

1. Please make sure your dog is <u>spayed/neutered</u>!

- It is still possible to alter an adult dog, yes.

- Just note that if you spay/neuter an **adult dog**, it may *temporarily* show some unpleasant behavioral changes, particularly in the first 3 to 12 months after the surgical intervention an increase in aggression (both towards animals and towards humans/you)

- However, this can be successfully controlled if you choose the right dog training approach, like the one we recommend and feature here, which is based on your <u>acceptance</u> as Pack leader

- For the latest advice on spaying/neutering see: mygermanshepherd.org/periodical/gsd-spaying-and-neutering

2. Please <u>do visit the vet regularly</u>. Once a year is the absolute minimum, because one year for us is between 6 and 12 years(!) for our dog (depending on breed, see mygermanshepherd.org/german-shepherd -age-how-old-does-my-dog-think-it-is). The best and cheapest outcome for us is then that each time the vet concludes: "Your dog is fine!"

3. However, please <u>do not simply nod through</u> every treatment a vet suggests. Our aim should always be to <u>get the correct diagnosis</u>, and to <u>then use the most</u>

appropriate treatment with the _least_ long-term side effects.

- A great example: The top ear infection remedy _Zymox Otic_ is available _with_ hydrocortisone and _without_ hydrocortisone.

- Hydrocortisone is a corticosteroid, a hormone, and as such it can have dramatic side effects with impact on seemingly unrelated body functions!

- Hence our priority should be to use Zymox Otic _without_ hydrocortisone: mygermanshepherd.org/go/ear-treatment-without-cortisone

4. Since we are at it, before you use any ear solution, you must get your dog's eardrums checked by a vet: If a solution is instilled into an ear canal with a perforated eardrum, it will enter the middle ear and damage structures essential to hearing! Then the solution is no 'solution' but a problem.

5. Always aim for antibiotic-free remedies.

- Do NOT get caught up in the myth that antibiotics are 'a generally suitable blanket treatment for infections'.

- No, antibiotics are a generally _unsuitable_ and typically _unnecessary_ treatment - and _always_ lead to chronic side effects that will sooner or later become apparent!

- Eg orally administered antibiotics impair the gastrointestinal wall, resulting in chronic excess gas and life-long intoxication of the blood stream (thus often shortened life)!

- Mark that: They are *anti*biotics - which means against life.

- For almost every condition there exist more effective natural remedies that have less side effects.

- The *only* exception to use antibiotics: a *life-threatening* condition of our dog.

Much more information on all the above points you can of course later find in the Health Compendium (mygermanshepherd.org/go/health-compendium).

6. Consider micro-chipping your dog (mygermanshepherd.org/periodical/micro-chipping-your-dog).
Particularly dogs of certain breeds are prone to get stolen with the purpose to sell them, or dognapped for various reasons. In any case (ie regardless where you live), dogs do commonly get lost often indeed!

7. Please do consider to get a dog from a rescue center/ shelter. - "Do not breed or buy while shelter dogs die!"

Did I forget other important points? Is there anything how this book could be improved?

Feedback much appreciated:
mailto: support@mygermanshepherd.org -
Will add to next edition!

Most importantly, a final note:

A Dog's Life is Fairly Short

so Make Sure You

ENJOY Your Dog! :-)

Every day is a new chance to put things right.

Connect with Tim Carter:
https://twitter.com/mygsdorg
http://mygermanshepherd.org/comments/feed/
https://smashwords.com/interview/TimCarter
https://www.goodreads.com/TimCarter
Questions only on the website (a page where it fits the content): http://mygermanshepherd.org

Lightning Source UK Ltd.
Milton Keynes UK
UKHW02f2107220118
316643UK00006B/642/P